INTERVIEWER
SUCCESS

BECOME A GREAT INTERVIEWER
IN LESS THAN ONE HOUR

By Amanda Haddaway

AmandaHaddaway.com

ISBN-13: 978-1482316148
ISBN-10: 1482316145

TABLE OF CONTENTS

WHY YOU NEED THIS GUIDE

At some point in your career, you will most likely be asked to interview a candidate for an open position within your organization. Perhaps you have an interview scheduled for this week and you need information now on how to interview someone without getting yourself in hot water or breaking the law.

Interviewing is a learned skill and doesn't always come naturally for people, so I've put together this quick guide to help you put the candidate at ease, find out the information that you need to know about the candidate, and make a good hiring decision.

Some managers and human resources professionals argue that recruiting (and in turn, interviewing) is one of the most essential business functions in their organizations. Whether you agree with this statement or not, the importance of interviewing should not be understated.

Recruiting has an impact on revenue, strategic goals, competitive advantage and organizational success. Success in these areas is paramount to having a healthy and successful business. Your role as an interviewer is extremely important, so you must know how to do this job well.

In fact, extensive research has been performed on the cost of a bad hire. According to a recent CareerBuilder survey of nearly 2,700 employers, 41 percent estimated that a single bad hire cost them more than $25,000, while a quarter of respondents said it cost more than $50,000. Yikes!

When you are a skilled interviewer, your company is more likely to make the right hires with better performance results. You will be praised for your business acumen.

In this guide, you will learn how to:

- Define what you're looking for in a candidate

- Review résumés to determine who should be brought in for an interview

- Prepare for an interview

- Set the tone for an interview and create a supportive communication climate for the candidate

- Listen better for understanding

- Look for non-verbal communication cues and body language

- Create interview questions that allow candidates to share their past performance

- Ask questions that elicit more than "yes or no" responses

- Handle special interviewing situations

- Ask only legal questions

- Use the information that you've gathered during the interview to make a hiring decision

Let's get started...

WHAT TYPE OF CANDIDATE DO YOU NEED?

Before you can begin the recruiting process, you must first know what type of person you need to hire. Your ultimate goal is to hire the best person for the job. In order to do this, you must understand the knowledge, skills and abilities it will take to be successful in the job and within your organization.

Depending on the size of your organization and your role, you may be tasked with writing the job description. If this is the case, make sure that you are as specific as possible on the job's duties and responsibilities.

Doing a good job with this initial step makes the rest of the recruitment process easier. Candidates use your job description as their main tool for deciding if they are interested and qualified for the position. For the candidate that you select, the job description also serves as the foundation for determining expected levels of performance.

Be honest in documenting the job title and duties. Make sure you're using gender-neutral and non-discriminatory language in your description, but accurately reflecting what you need in order for the hire to be successful.

Include information on the work hours or schedule, location of the job, required and desired skills, and educational requirements (if applicable). If the position has physical demands or uncommon working conditions, that information should also be included in the job description. Your job description may include subject-matter expertise, as well as "soft skills." For example, if the position requires strong written communication skills or experience in customer service, make sure that is included in the description.

It's also helpful to include a paragraph or two about your organization and anything in the corporate culture that is unique or different. When writing this section, try to answer "Why would someone want to work here?" and "What makes us an employer of choice?"

If your organization has a human resources person or department, have someone review your draft description to ensure that the information that you've included is legal and clearly represents your employer.

If you don't know where to start with this process, visit the O*NET website and enter a keyword or series of keywords to find sample tasks for thousands of jobs. You can also visit popular online recruitment sites like Monster and CareerBuilder to see what other companies are using as their job descriptions.

Once the position description is completed, the next phase of the recruitment process can begin. You, or someone in your organization, will advertise the position and hopefully receive lots of qualified candidates who are interested in working for you. Since this guide is for interviewers, we won't cover that part of the process in this guide. We can now move forward to reviewing résumés.

HOW TO REVIEW A RÉSUMÉ

In our last step, we wrote the job description and defined what we're looking for in the perfect candidate. Now, we must revisit that description and compare and contrast it to the résumés that we've received.

So, what should you look for on a résumé?

You'll want to pay particular attention to the person's skills and how they compare with the skills required in your job opening. Is the person a perfect match? Do they have some skills that are the same? Are their skills in a totally different subject area?

You will most likely receive some résumés that are not anywhere remotely close to what you need for your opening. If that's the case, put them in the "not interviewing now" pile. Next, determine which of the candidates having some of the required skills could get up to speed for your position with a little training. These résumés should go on the "maybe" pile.

Now, take a second look at the résumés that you initially thought were a good match. If you have a lot in this pile, you'll need to be more discerning since you probably don't have time to interview large numbers of candidates. Go through these résumés with a fine-tooth comb and try to obtain as much information from the résumé as possible. Does the candidate have the level of experience that the position requires?

Also look for "red flags" on the résumé. Red flags are items that may cause an employer concern. For example, the candidate has many employers and has only stayed with each employer for a few months. This could be a sign that the person has trouble maintaining steady employment. Also look for gaps in employment. Although these items don't necessarily indicate a problem, they do require further questioning during a pre-interview screen of the candidate.

If your corporate culture requires a lot of team work and inter-action, look for items on the résumé that indicate whether the candidate worked independently or with others. It may be hard to assess soft skills like problem-solving and communication from the résumé alone, but look for previous performance indicators in these areas if they are important to your position.

Once you select some of the candidates for interviews, we're ready to prepare for the interview.

PREPARING FOR
THE INTERVIEW

One of the best ways to prepare for an interview is to set some time aside the day before or a few hours before the actual candidate arrives. This time should be used to review the position description again and remind yourself of the essential job skills, as well as the "nice to have" job skills.

Take a few minutes and think about your best interviewing experience and your worst interviewing experience. What were the characteristics of each situation? Why does one stand out in your memory as being the best? What was so bad about your worst experience?

Think about both of these experiences each time you prepare for an interview. Consider what you will do to make the interview experience a best interview memory for the candidate instead of a worst interview memory.

You should also do a thorough review of the candidate's résumé. Use a separate notebook to jot down any questions that you might have about the candidate's previous experience. We'll talk more about creating actual interview questions in a later section of this guide, but go ahead and write down any comments or concerns that you want to make sure you bring up during the interview. If there are any red flag items, be sure you leave yourself a reminder note to ask about those items.

It's helpful to print a copy of the position description and the candidate's résumé, so that you have easy access to this information during the interview. Make sure you have note paper and a pen available as well to take notes during your interview. This is especially important if you have more than one interview scheduled in a day. You'll want to be certain that you remember the differences between the candidates when you go to make a hiring decision.

Depending on your organization's interviewing policies, you may be required to submit an interview comment sheet that details your discussion with the candidate. It is important to document your conversation accurately because this data will be included in the hiring packet and could be subject to an audit.

If the interview is going to take place in your office, ensure that your workspace is tidy. As the interviewer, it's your responsibility to make the candidate feel at ease. It's hard to feel at ease when a candidate has to climb over or move piles of paperwork in order to have a seat in your office.

If your workspace is shared or not private, consider finding an alternate location for the interview. A smaller conference room is a perfect choice. If space like this doesn't exist in your organization, you might consider meeting at a location outside of your workplace that is quiet and professional. The candidate needs enough personal space to feel comfortable during the interview.

Most interviews last between a half hour and one hour depending on the level and complexity of the position. Candidates who are asked to interview for a half-day or more often experience "interviewer fatigue" and don't perform at their best. Keep this in mind when you're scheduling interviews.

SETTING THE TONE FOR AN INTERVIEW AND CREATING A SUPPORTIVE COMMUNICATION CLIMATE FOR THE CANDIDATE

For some candidates, interviewing ranks right up there with getting a root canal – they find the entire experience to be gut-wrenching. Your goal as an interviewer is to put the candidate at ease. One of the best ways to do this is to start your conversation with some ice breaker questions. My go-to question is "Did you have any problems finding our office?" This question isn't too personal and it gives the candidate a chance to answer a question without having to prove that he is qualified for the position from the second the interview begins. One caution on ice breakers: Make sure that your question isn't too personal. We'll talk more about illegal interview questions later in this guide, but keep in mind that your questions should generally stick to job-related information or details about your organization.

Once you're seated in your interview location, explain to the candidate what he or she should expect. This is your opportunity to set the tone for the interview and guide the conversation.

You may want to tell the candidate how long the interview will take and mention that you will be taking notes as the interview goes along. Let the candidate know that there will be an opportunity to ask questions at the end of your interview.

LISTENING BETTER FOR UNDERSTANDING

In an interview, listening may be even more important than speaking. You will be basing your hiring decision on what the candidate tells you in a very short period of time. It is critical to pay attention to what the candidate is saying through active listening.

Active listening requires you to be present in the situation, focused on the candidate and free from other distractions. Although our computers and cell phones are very important, there is no place for them during an interview.

If you find yourself often distracted by email or other technology devices, leave them elsewhere during the interview or turn them off. The candidate deserves your undivided attention. There is nothing worse than talking to someone who keeps looking at a computer monitor and doesn't seem interested in what you're saying. Keep in mind that an interview also has a sales component. That is, you are selling your organization as much as the candidate is selling himself to you. Would you want to work for someone who acts like what you are saying isn't important? Probably not.

Reflective listening is also a great technique to use during an interview. Essentially, you listen to what the candidate is saying and then paraphrase in your own words to demonstrate your understanding. Make sure you're not sounding like a parrot and repeating the candidate verbatim.

If you are unclear on what the candidate is saying, ask follow-up questions to obtain further understanding. It's totally acceptable to delve a little deeper into what the candidate answers initially if this is information that's going to help you make a hiring decision.

LOOKING FOR NON-VERBAL COMMUNICATION CUES AND BODY LANGUAGE

Research has shown that only 20 percent of communication is contained in the conversation's actual words. The remaining 80 percent comes from tone of voice and other non-verbal cues.

Body language provides important insights into the meaning behind a person's words. Astute observers of body language may be able to detect when there is a discrepancy between a non-verbal cue and what a candidate is actually saying. Body language may be expressed through facial expressions, eye contact, gestures, physical contact, personal space and posture.

If a candidate exhibits closed or defensive behavior, it might be a sign that the candidate is anxious, nervous or stressed. These are all common feelings for candidates who are interviewing. If you notice these behaviors, consider using some additional ice breaker questions to help the person relax.

You may also notice that a candidate leans forward or nods and smiles when you speak. The candidate is demonstrating responsive non-verbal communication. The candidate may feel comfortable and relaxed with you or in agreement with what you are saying.

It's important to understand and be comfortable with brief pauses and short periods of silence during an interview. Once you ask questions, candidates may pause to collect their thoughts before responding. There may also be silence as you take notes based on what the candidate says. We have a tendency to want to fill these voids. Try not to jump in with additional comments while the candidate is pausing to respond. If the silence goes on for more than 30 seconds, you might consider rephrasing the question in a different way to make sure that you were understood.

The various forms of body language can help you extract deeper meaning from the interview conversation.

CREATING INTERVIEW QUESTIONS THAT ALLOW CANDIDATES TO SHARE THEIR PAST PERFORMANCE

All of the questions that you develop should be based on the job and the person's résumé and not on your own personal biases. If the question does not pertain to the job and job functions, you probably shouldn't be asking it.

One of the most successful interviewing techniques is behavioral interviewing. The idea behind behavioral interviewing is that past behavior predicts future performance. Behavioral interviewing is a way to collect and analyze data and examples of how someone has performed in similar situations in the past. This past performance can help predict how the candidate will perform in the job that you are trying to fill.

There are several benefits from using behavioral interviewing techniques. The primary benefit is that candidates usually can't fake it. That is, in order to answer the questions that you are asking, the candidate must rely on previous experience. You'll find out if the person truly has the experience necessary to be successful in your position.

What a candidate has actually done is a much better indicator of future job success than what a candidate believes, feels or thinks. Behavioral-based questions are useful in getting candidates to discuss work realities rather than notions and suppositions.

Furthermore, behavioral interviewing is a systematic process that shows candidates you're serious about managing talent. It forces the interviewer to do the work of interviewing and not just regurgitate what's on the résumé.

As you develop questions, remember the knowledge, skills and abilities necessary for the position. If your questions are formed properly, you'll be able to determine if the candidate truly has the experience that was listed on the résumé and whether or not the candidate will be a good fit for the job. Consider, too, asking questions about soft skills to determine if the person has motivation and the ability to follow through on tasks.

Your questions should be open-ended. You should not ask questions that require only a "yes or no" response without any additional information.

The first few questions should set the stage and put the candidate at ease. Remember to have an ice breaker question when you first greet the candidate. You shouldn't start the interview with your toughest interview question. Work up to the tougher questions as your conversation proceeds.

Make sure you avoid leading questions that can inject bias into a response. For example, if you are concerned about the person's ability to work long hours, you might say:

"This position requires hours outside of the normal 8-5. Are you able to work additional hours outside of your regular schedule."

You would not want to say:

"This position requires hours outside of the normal 8-5. Since you are a single parent with young children, I hope that won't be a problem."

We'll talk more about illegal questions in a future section of this guide, but this example gives you a taste for how bias could enter into a question.

Since you're preparing your interview questions in advance, it will be easy to ask the same questions of all candidates to ensure fairness across the interview process. Although you're not expected to be an interviewer robot, you should try to be consistent in your line of questioning for all candidates.

Behavioral interview questions are framed in a very specific format. The candidate is asked to provide a situation where they took an action and performed a task. The candidate is then expected to share the result of that situation. This format is commonly referred to as the STAR method.

Situation

Task

Action

Result

Questions are generally asked in one of these formats:

- Tell me about a time when...

- Give me an example of a time when...

- Describe a time when...

Several examples of questions in this format are included on page 38 of this guide.

If a candidate is not able to articulate the situation, task, action and result in an answer, you may need to probe for additional details. It is acceptable to ask for clarification and additional details to ensure that you fully understand the candidate's answer. Making a hiring decision is a tough and important choice, so make sure you know as much about the candidate's knowledge, skills and abilities as possible.

ASKING QUESTIONS THAT ELICIT MORE THAN "YES OR NO" RESPONSES

For novice interviewers, it's easy to fall into the trap of just asking questions or confirming data from the candidate's résumé. For example:

> "I see you worked for XYZ Company as a human resources manager."

> "Oh, I see you were responsible for writing the employee handbook."

These really aren't questions and only require the candidate to say "yes" or nod. This type of statement doesn't obtain any additional information about the candidate's ability to be successful in your position.

What if you asked a behavioral-based question instead? For example:

> "Tell me about a time when you had to discipline an employee."

"Give me an example of a time when you had to conform to a policy with which you didn't agree."

"Describe a time when you had to use your presentation skills to influence someone's opinion."

The responses from the behavioral questions require much more than one word responses. In fact, you'll have insight into what the candidate was responsible for and how those very same skills could translate into your organization.

Interviewers sometimes feel awkward when they start using behavioral interviewing techniques. The best way to overcome this is to plan out your questions before the interview and have a written copy with you. You'll also find yourself becoming more comfortable with practice of these techniques.

In fact, you might even start using these question formats in your personal life with your significant other, contractors who are doing home repairs, your children and other people with whom you interact. You'll be amazed at how much additional information you can obtain by simply rephrasing your questions into the behavioral-based format.

ASKING ONLY LEGAL QUESTIONS

The responsibility of interviewing shouldn't be minimized. There are countless employment lawsuits on the books relating to interviewers asking illegal questions and, in turn, getting sued by candidates who felt wronged. These are situations that we all want to avoid, so it's important to understand what can and cannot be asked in an interview.

You'll remember that earlier in this guide, I said that questions should relate to the job. Always keep this tip in your mind when you are interviewing a candidate.

You should be aware of Equal Employment Opportunity laws and regulations. These federal and, in many cases, state laws prohibit discrimination against candidates on the basis of age, race, color, religion, gender, disability and national origin. There are also laws that prohibit discrimination against women who are pregnant and the use of genetic information in hiring decisions. If your organization has a human resources department, someone should be able to provide you information on the employment laws that pertain to your organization. If you are a smaller business without an HR person, there are many resources available online, including the Equal Employment Opportunity Commission's website.

The following is a list of topics with both legal and discriminatory questions. Although you may ask the legal questions, only use them if they pertain to the job requirements.

FAMILY STATUS:

Legal question: Do you have any responsibilities that conflict with attendance or travel requirements?

Why this question is legal: The position requires the person filling the job to have regular attendance and the ability to travel. This question pertains to the job duties.

Discriminatory questions: Are you married? Do you have children? Are you pregnant?

Why these questions are illegal: The questions have no bearing on whether or not the person can perform the job.

RACE:

Legal question: None.

Discriminatory question: What is your race?

Why this question is illegal: The EEOC protects people from discrimination based on race. A person's race does not impact one's ability to do a job.

RELIGION:

Legal question: None.

Discriminatory questions: What church do you attend? What is your religion?

Why these questions are illegal: The EEOC protects people from discrimination based on religion. A person's religion does not impact one's ability to do a job.

RESIDENCE:

Legal question: What is your address?

Why this question is legal: Prospective employers may ask a candidate's address to correspond with the person during the interviewing process.

Illegal questions: Do you own your home? Do you rent your home? Who lives with you?

Why these questions are illegal: A person's residence has no bearing on whether or not he or she will be a good employee.

GENDER:

Legal question: None.

Discriminatory question: Are you male or female?

Why this question is illegal: The EEOC protects people from discrimination based on gender. A person's gender does not impact one's ability to do a job.

AGE:

Legal question: If you are hired, can you provide proof that you are at least 18?

Why this question is legal: Some employers are only able to hire candidates who are legally adults. If this does not apply to your workplace, you shouldn't ask this question.

Discriminatory questions: How old are you? When is your birth date?

Why these questions are illegal: The EEOC protects people from discrimination based on age. A person's age does not impact one's ability to do a job.

Interviewers are allowed to ask candidates if they have ever been convicted of a crime, but they may not ask if they have been arrested. You must also state that the conviction will be considered only as it relates to the ability to do the job. For example, many positions require security clearances. Depending on the type of convictions, the person may have difficulty in obtaining a security clearance.

You may also ask if a candidate can show proof of eligibility to work in the United States and if the candidate is fluent in any other languages other than English. However, you may not ask if the person is a U.S. citizen or where a candidate was born.

Many organizations have application forms that are used when a candidate arrives for an interview. Many of these legal questions can be put on the application form so that the interviewer isn't burdened with walking on a slippery slope of legal versus discriminatory questioning. If your organization has an HR department, ask if there is an application form and if you may see a copy. If your organization doesn't have an HR person or department, there are several vendors, including most office supply stores, who sell ready-made application forms that meet legal criteria.

HANDLING SPECIAL INTERVIEWING SITUATIONS

CANDIDATES WITH DISABILITIES

The Americans with Disabilities Act (ADA) affects every employer with 15 or more employees. The intent of this law is to prohibit discrimination against qualified people with disabilities. Employers may not screen out candidates solely on their disabilities.

The interview process should be handled the same way for people with and without disabilities. Because you may not know if a candidate has a disability before the person arrives to the interview, always have a plan B.

Make sure your interview space is accessible to people with various types of disabilities. It is important that you treat a disabled candidate the same way that you would treat a non-disabled candidate. Don't focus on the person's disability or assume that the person needs extra assistance, but be prepared to help should you be asked.

Keep in mind that not all disabilities are visible. Interviewers are able to ask if the candidate can perform the essential functions of the job with or without reasonable accommodation. Conversely, the interviewer may not ask if the candidate is disabled or about the nature or severity of a disability.

You may encounter other strange interviewing situations. For example, I once had a candidate who became ill during the interview process. There are no steadfast rules on how to handle this type of situation, but make sure that you treat the candidate with respect and dignity. One possible solution is to reschedule the interview for an alternate time.

TELEPHONE INTERVIEWS

In some instances, candidates can't be physically in the same room with you for an interview. Here are my top tips for phone interviews:

1. Treat the phone interview the same way that you would an in-person job interview. This means that you should be focused and come prepared with knowledge of both the candidate and the job.

2. If you must take the call from your cell phone, make sure that you are in an area that has good reception and you're in a quiet environment. Background noises are very distracting.

3. Eliminate any distractions while on the phone. Some interviewers find that they focus better when they are not interviewing in their own offices.

4. Telephone interviews don't allow for eye contact and body language, so interviewers must ensure that they

fully understand the verbal answers that are provided by the candidate. If this is a concern, determine if a video interview is a viable alternative.

USING THE INFORMATION THAT YOU'VE GATHERED DURING THE INTERVIEW TO MAKE A HIRING DECISION

You're almost finished! Now what?

Ideally, you will have collected enough quality information from the interview that you can determine whether or not you want to extend an offer to a candidate. Your organization may ask you to complete an interview comment sheet to document your discussion with the candidate and show how you've come to your hiring decision. If this is the case, make sure that your documented comments are only about the knowledge, skills and abilities of the candidate. Make sure that you don't include comments including your personal biases. Interview comments may be subject to audit at a later date.

At a minimum, you need to work with the people in your organization who are responsible for notifying the candidate of your decision. If that person is you, make sure that you follow-up with all candidates who interviewed in a reasonable amount of time and let them know your hiring decision. As a job-seeker, there's nothing worse than waiting to hear results from a company, but hearing nothing for weeks after the interview. If that company doesn't have a formal notification in place, the candidate is left wondering what happened and that's not a fair way to treat people who took time to meet with you about your opening.

Your organization probably has a process in place for extending offers of employment. Most organizations use a written letter that includes information about the job, its location, schedule, starting salary, benefits and so forth.

Once a candidate accepts your offer, pat yourself on the back for successfully completing the recruiting process. Like many skills, practice makes perfect. You'll be better prepared the next time you need to interview candidates for another opening.

50 SAMPLE INTERVIEW QUESTIONS

Feel free to use these questions during your next interview. You may be surprised how much information you can collect by rephrasing your questions from the standard résumé regurgitation drill.

Although there are 50 sample questions, you will probably only need a small portion of this list for most interviews. Review the questions and select the ones that are most relevant to the position that you are trying to fill. You can also create your own questions using the format described on page 25 of this workbook.

1. Tell me about a time when you had to discipline an employee.

2. Give me an example of a time when you had to conform to a policy with which you didn't agree.

3. Describe a time when you had to use your presentation skills to influence someone's opinion.

4. Describe a situation in which you were able to use persuasion to successfully convince someone to see things your way.

5. Describe a time when you were faced with a stressful situation that demonstrated your coping skills.

6. Give me a specific example of a time when you used good judgment and logic in solving a problem.

7. Give me an example of a time when you set a goal and were able to meet or achieve it.

8. Tell me about a time when you had to go above and beyond the call of duty in order to get a job done.

9. Tell me about a time when you had too many things to do and you were required to prioritize your tasks.

10. Give me an example of a time when you had to make a split-second decision.

11. What is your typical way of dealing with conflict? Give me an example.

12. Tell me about a time when you were able to successfully deal with another person even when that individual may not have personally liked you (or vice versa).

13. Give me an example of a time when something you tried to accomplish ended in failure.

14. Give me an example of when you showed initiative and took the lead.

15. Tell me about a recent situation in which you had to deal with a very upset customer or co-worker.

16. Give me an example of a time when you motivated others.

17. Tell me about a time when you delegated a project effectively.

18. Give me an example of a time when you used your fact-finding skills to solve a problem.

19. Tell me about a time when you missed an obvious solution to a problem.

20. Describe a time when you anticipated potential problems and developed preventative measures.

21. Tell me about a time when you were forced to make an unpopular decision.

22. Please describe your present responsibilities and duties.

23. What are the kinds of things you particularly enjoy in your present position? What things do you enjoy least?

24. What do you consider to have been your major accomplishments?

25. In regards to your present employment, have you had any disappointments or things that turned out less than expected? Tell me about them.

26. In what ways has your present job changed since you were originally hired?

27. What are your reasons for wanting to leave your present employment?

28. In the past, for what things have your supervisors complimented you? For what have they criticized you? How do you think your present supervisor would describe you?

29. How would you describe your relationship with the managers, co-workers and/or clients with whom you work?

30. What are some of the things you find difficult to do?

31. In what ways has your present job prepared you for greater responsibilities?

32. What do you feel is the most important function of a _____ (job title)?

33. As you see it, what would be some advantages to you if you were to obtain this position with this organization?

34. What disadvantages or drawbacks might there be?

35. In what ways does this position meet your career goals and objectives?

36. What do you regard as your outstanding qualities? What do you regard as some of your shortcomings?

37. What has contributed to your career success up to the present time?

38. What are your long-range goals and objectives?

39. What are some of the things that are important to you in a job?

40. Tell me how you increased teamwork among a previous group with whom you worked.

41. Describe what you liked and disliked about how you were managed in previous positions.

42. Recall a time when you made what you consider a mistake or a bad decision on the job. How did you handle the situation?

43. In your past work life, what kind of co-workers or clients rubbed you the wrong way? How did you respond?

44. Tell me about a time when you set specific work goals for yourself. How did things turn out?

45. Walk me through the major highlights of your career so far and tell me where you want to go next.

46. In your most recent position, what did you learn? How did you apply this learning?

47. Every manager has to learn to delegate well. Describe a work situation in which you delegated responsibility successfully. Then tell me about a time when your delegation of responsibility did not work out well. How did you handle that situation?

48. What approaches worked best for you in the past in communicating with your boss? With your co-workers? With your subordinates?

49. Tell me about a time when you took charge as a leader in a work situation without being formally assigned to that role by your boss.

50. Tell me about a time when you felt you went beyond the call of duty in helping a client.

NOTES

_____

_____

_____

_____

_____

_____

_____

_____

_____

_____

_____

_____

ABOUT THE AUTHOR

 Amanda Haddaway is a recognized career expert and leader in the human resources field, as well as being an accomplished writer and marketing practitioner. She has been quoted in numerous national publications for her HR and marketing expertise and has written her own book, *Destination Real World: Success after Graduation* for new and soon-to-be college graduates.

Over the past decade, Amanda has worked in many facets of human resources and marketing, including recruiting, training, employee communications, corporate compliance, social media and advertising campaign development. She currently serves as the director of human resources and marketing for Folcomer Equipment Corporation, a multi-state construction equipment dealership. Prior to her employment at Folcomer Equipment, Amanda worked for SRA International, a Fortune 100 Best Company to Work For.

Amanda holds a master's degree from the George Washington University and a bachelor's degree from James Madison University.

For additional information or to contact Amanda, please visit AmandaHaddaway.com.

Photo credit: Mary Kate McKenna Photography